Editor
Eric Migliaccio

Managing Editor
Ina Massler Levin, M.A.

Editor-in-Chief
Sharon Coan, M.S. Ed.

Illustrator
L. Renee Camargo

Cover Artist
Janet Chadwick

Art Coordinator
Kevin Barnes

Art Director
CJae Froshay

Imaging
Rosa C. See

Product Manager
Phil Garcia

Publisher
Mary D. Smith, M.S. Ed.

GRADE 4

Author

Debra J. Housel, M.S. Ed.

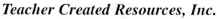

Teacher Created Resources, Inc.
6421 Industry Way
Westminster, CA 92683
www.teachercreated.com
ISBN: 978-0-7439-3774-0
©2003 Teacher Created Resources, Inc.
Reprinted, 2012
Made in U.S.A.

Table of Contents

Introduction

The old adage "practice makes perfect" can really hold true for your child's education. The more practice and exposure your child has with concepts being taught in school, the more success he or she is likely to find. For many parents, knowing how to help their children may be frustrating because the resources may not be readily available. As a parent, it is also difficult to know where to focus your efforts so that the extra practice your child receives at home supports what he or she is learning in school.

This book has been written to help parents and teachers reinforce basic skills with children. *Practice Makes Perfect: Spelling* covers basic spelling skills for fourth graders. The exercises in this book can be completed in any order. The practice included in this book will meet or reinforce educational standards and objectives similar to the ones required by your state and school district for fourth graders:

- The student will know three-consonant clusters' sounds and spellings.

- The student will recognize the spelling patterns for silent letters.

- The student will recognize the pronunciation and spelling patterns for common word parts.

- The student will know how to write plurals, including unusual plurals.

- The student will spell verbs ending in "ed" and "ing."

- The student will spell high-frequency words, the 3,000 words that make up more than 90 percent of all written material. The majority of the words in these spelling lessons are these high-frequency words.

How to Make the Most of this Book

Here are some ideas for making the most of this book:

- Set aside a specific place in your home to work on this book. Keep it neat and tidy, with the necessary materials on hand.

- Determine a specific time of day to work on these practice pages in order to establish consistency. Look for times in your day or week that are less hectic and more conducive to practicing skills.

- Keep all practice sessions with your child positive and constructive. If your child becomes frustrated or tense, set aside the book and look for another time to practice. Forcing your child to perform will not help. Do not use this book as a punishment.

- Review and praise the work your child has done.

- Introduce the spelling words in the list. Discuss how the words are different and how they are alike. Read the "In Context" column together. Be sure that the students understand the meaning of each word.

- If necessary, help the student to read and comprehend the directions and exercises.

- Encourage the child to point out spelling words, past and present, in the books, newspapers, and magazines he or she reads.

Months and Time

Here are some important words about time:

Word	In Context
o'clock	I will pick you up at seven **o'clock**.
decade (*ten years*)	Have you been alive for a **decade**?
century (*100 years*)	Will you live for a **century**?
January	New Year's Day is in **January**.
February	Valentine's Day is in **February**.
March	Spring starts near the end of **March**.
April	April Fool's Day is on **April** 1.
May	Memorial Day is the last Monday of **May**.
June	Flag Day is celebrated **June** 14.
July	We often see fireworks on the Fourth of **July**.
August	**August** brings the end of summer vacation.
September	Many children start school in **September**.
October	Columbus Day is in **October**.
November	Thanksgiving Day is in **November**.
December	The last month of the year is **December**.

Is the **boldfaced** word spelled wrong? If it is not correct, write it correctly in the middle column. If it is correct, circle OK.

1. Is your birthday in **August**?		OK
2. He was born on the first of **May**.		OK
3. Meet me at the park at two **oclock**.		OK
4. The longest day of the year is in **June**.		OK
5. Does Easter come in **March** this year?		OK
6. We had a big snowstorm last **Febuary**.		OK
7. The shortest day of the year is in **December**.		OK
8. They moved out of that house more than a **decad** ago.		OK
9. She plans to visit us in **November**.		OK
10. Labor Day is the first Monday of **Setember**.		OK
11. The U.S. became a nation during the 18th **centery**.		OK
12. They plan to get married this **October**.		OK
13. **April** is the first month of spring.		OK
14. The first month of the year is **Janary**.		OK
15. It's usually hot here during **Jully**.		OK

Months and Time *(cont.)*

Crossword Puzzle

Choose the spelling word that would best complete each clue. When you're done, go back and put the letters that should be capitalized in red pen.

Across

1. A set of ten years is called a _____ .
8. A _____ is 100 years long.
9. My family eats dinner at six _____ .
11. Summer begins in the month of _____ .
13. Presidents' Day is celebrated in the month of _____ .
14. Autumn begins in the third week of _____ .
15. Some people celebrate Halloween at the end of _____ .

Down

2. _____ showers bring May flowers.
3. A day in _____ is set aside to honor Dr. Martin Luther King, Jr.
4. The month before June is_____ .
5. Christmas is celebrated in the month of _____ .
6. The seventh month of the year is _____ .
7. Veterans Day is celebrated in the month of _____ .
10. The eighth month of the year is _____ .
12. _____ comes in like a lion and goes out like a lamb.

Consonant Clusters: "thr," "spr," "shr"

Consonant clusters are sets of three letters that appear together, usually at the beginning of a word. You hear the sound of each separate letter in "spr." However, "thr" and "shr" both contain digraphs. For "thr" and "shr" you hear the digraph's sound followed by "r."

Word	In Context
thread	I can't seem to **thread** this needle.
thrill	What's the best **thrill** ride you've ever been on?
throat	She is out today with a sore **throat**.
through	Pass **through** the gates, then turn to your left.
throughout	These signs have appeared **throughout** the city.
spruce	We used a large **spruce** for our Christmas tree.
sprain	If she trips over those roots, she might **sprain** an ankle.
sprawl	Someone might trip over you if you **sprawl** on the floor.
sprout	The pumpkin seeds began to **sprout** last week.
spread	Please **spread** out the photos for us to see.
shrubs	He hid behind the **shrubs**.
shriek	She was so scared that she made a loud **shriek**.
shrink	If you wash wool in hot water, it will **shrink**.
shrimp	They plan to order **shrimp.**
shred	We can **shred** the cabbage and lettuce for the salad.

Write the spelling words that rhyme with the same sound as the word given. Each spelling word is used just once.

ex.	bet
	threat

about	fed	limp	blink

goat	loose	drain	clubs

blew	spill	crawl	peek

Consonant Clusters: "thr," "spr," "shr" (cont.)

Word Scramble

Unscramble the words below to form spelling words from this lesson. Put the letters on the lines at the bottom to find the answer to the riddle.

Example: trnoeh   <u>t</u>   <u>h</u>   <u>r</u>   <u>o</u>   <u>n</u>   <u>e</u>
            1

1. ottrah   ___ ___ ___ ___ ___ ___
               2

2. upserc   ___ ___ ___ ___ ___
           3

3. ouptsr   ___ ___ ___ ___ ___
                4

4. drapes*   ___ ___ ___ ___ ___ ___
              5

5. msphir   ___ ___ ___ ___ ___ ___
       6

6. inspar   ___ ___ ___ ___ ___ ___
              7

7. radeth   ___ ___ ___ ___ ___ ___
      8

8. skreih   ___ ___ ___ ___ ___ ___
           9

9. drehs   ___ ___ ___ ___ ___
         10

10. ltirhl   ___ ___ ___ ___ ___ ___
            11

11. srsuhb   ___ ___ ___ ___ ___ ___
     12

12. wrapsl   ___ ___ ___ ___ ___ ___
           13

13. hhugrot   ___ ___ ___ ___ ___ ___ ___
          14   15

14. krinsh   ___ ___ ___ ___ ___ ___
   16

15. oughrthotu   ___ ___ ___ ___ ___ ___ ___ ___ ___ ___
          17   18

*This is already a word, but please rearrange the letters to form a spelling word from this lesson.

Riddle: Which heavenly bodies must follow hunting laws?

___ ___ ___   <u>t</u> ___ ___   ___ ___ ___ ___ ___ ___ ___ ___   ___ ___ ___ ___ s!
5   11   13   1   12   10   6   15   17   18   4   9   7   14   16   8   2   3

Consonant Clusters: "spl" & "str"

Consonant clusters are sets of three letters that appear together, usually at the beginning of a word. You hear the sound of each letter in "spl" and "str."

Word	In Context
split	The walnut **split** in two.
splash	Please don't **splash** water in my face.
splinter	You need to get that **splinter** out of your hand.
splendid	It was a **splendid**, sunny day.
strong	My dad is so **strong** that he can carry a couch all by himself.
string	Use some **string** to tie the box shut.
strange	Last night she had a very **strange** dream.
stream	The children loved to turn over rocks in the **stream**.
strike	You shouldn't **strike** your brothers or sisters.
stress	He's been under a lot of **stress** lately.
stripes	The USA's flag has red and white **stripes**.
street	Which **street** do you live on?
struggle	Mark started to **struggle** against his seat belt.
straight	Shari has **straight** hair.
strength	All my **strength** seemed to be gone.

Copy the spelling words in the order they appear above. Make the changes. Write the new word. Did the vowel sound change?

Spelling Word	Change	New Word	Changed Sound?
ex. strap	replace "str" with "fl"	flap	no
1.	drop "p"		
2.	replace "spl" with "w"		
3.	replace "spl" with "w"		
4.	drop "did" add "e" before "n"		
5.	replace "str" with "am"		
6.	replace "i" with "un"		
7.	drop "st"		
8.	drop "r"		
9.	replace "str" with "b"		
10.	replace "str" with "l"		
11.	drop "e"		
12.	replace "str" with "m"		
13.	replace "u" with "a"		
14.	replace "stra" with "e"		
15.	replace "str" with "l"		

Challenge: Can you think of a sentence for each spelling word that uses both the spelling word *and* its new word? *Ex.* The loose <u>strap</u> began to <u>flap</u> in the wind.

Consonant Clusters: "spl" & "str" *(cont.)*

Finding Synonyms

Look up each spelling word in a dictionary or a thesaurus (if available). Find its synonym (word that means almost the same thing). Then write each spelling word on the line next to its synonym(s). Some list multiple synonyms to help you choose the best word.

Synonym(s)	Spelling Word
1. shatter	
2. road	
3. twine	
4. anxiety	
5. orderly; even; proper	
6. powerful; mighty	
7. brook	
8. lines	
9. fight	
10. spray	
11. wonderful	
12. hit	
13. skill; ability	
14. tear	
15. odd	

Consonant Clusters: "squ," "scr," "sch"

Consonant clusters are sets of three letters that appear together, usually at the beginning of a word. You hear the sound of each letter in "scr." However, "squ" says "skw" and "sch" says "sk."

Word	In Context
squeak	I could hear the mouse **squeak**, but I couldn't see the animal.
squeal	We heard the truck's brakes **squeal**.
squeeze	Be sure to **squeeze** the tube carefully.
squirm	The speech took so long that the child started to **squirm** in his seat.
squirt	Let's use our **squirt** guns.
squirrel	The **squirrel** gathered seeds and nuts for the winter.
scream	Did you just hear that awful **scream**?
screen	The TV **screen** went blank.
scribble	If you **scribble**, no one will be able to read your writing.
scrub	It's time to **scrub** the bathroom floor.
scrambled	After he **scrambled** the pieces, he put the puzzle back together.
scraps	Our dog always ate **scraps** from the table.
screech	We heard an owl **screech**.
scheme (plan, idea)	She has a new **scheme** for making money.
schedule	I'll see if I can fit it into my **schedule**.

Decode the cryptograms to form the spelling words above. Use the example to help you crack the code.

ex. pyowqyeba   <u>scratched</u>

1. pyobwj   _____
2. pnrbwh   _____
3. pyobbye   _____
4. pnrfoobh   _____
5. pyorx   _____
6. pyowmp   _____
7. pnrbbub   _____
8. pyebjb   _____
9. pyebarhb   _____
10. pyobbk   _____
11. pnrfoq   _____
12. pnrbwz   _____
13. pyofxxhb   _____
14. pnrfoj   _____
15. pyowjxhba   _____

Consonant Clusters: "squ," "scr," "sch" *(cont.)*

Pen Caps

Look at the letters on the body of each pen. On each pen cap write the appropriate consonant cluster (**squ**, **scr**, or **sch**) to form a spelling word from this lesson. Then write the whole word on the line. The first one has been done for you.

1. squ | eeze | squeeze
2. | eme |
3. | irrel |
4. | ibble |
5. | edule |
6. | eech |
7. | eak |
8. | ub |
9. | irm |
10. | eam |
11. | aps |
12. | eal |
13. | een |
14. | ambled |
15. | irt |

11

Adding "ed" to Verbs

Here are a few rules to follow when making a verb past tense:
- To form the past tense, add "ed" to a verb (action word).
- If the word already ends with an "e," simply add a "d."
- If the final letters in the word are a short vowel followed by a consonant, double the consonant, then add "ed."

Word	Base + Ending	In Context
happened	happen + ed	I just **happened** to be walking past the store.
laughed	laugh + ed	The teens **laughed** at the joke.
developed	develop + ed	We got the film **developed** last week.
finished	finish + ed	They haven't **finished** their homework yet.
passed	pass + ed	She **passed** the first two houses and entered the third.
decided	decide + d	He **decided** to become a painter.
raised	raise + d	They **raised** chickens on their farm.
required	require + d	A fee of $30 is **required**.
prepared	prepare + d	Are you **prepared** for your trip?
arrived	arrive + d	The plane **arrived** right on time.
snapped	snap + ed	The pieces of the toy **snapped** together easily.
nodded	nod + ed	To show my agreement, I **nodded**.
slipped	slip + ed	The old lady **slipped** and fell down the steps.
rubbed	rub + ed	I **rubbed** my elbow where it had hit the door.
equipped	equip + ed	The boat was **equipped** with an expensive sound system.

Circle the word that's spelled correctly. Copy it on the line.

1. laffed   lauphed   laughed   _____
2. pepaired   prepared   preparred   _____
3. arrivved   arriveed   arrived   _____
4. happened   hapened   happenned   _____
5. requird   requireed   required   _____
6. raysed   raised   rased   _____
7. snapped   snaped   snapd   _____
8. decided   desided   descided   _____
9. noded   nodd   nodded   _____
10. sliped   slippd   slipped   _____
11. finished   finnished   finishhed   _____
12. discoverred   discovered   discoverd   _____
13. equiped   equipped   equipt   _____
14. rubed   rubd   rubbed   _____
15. developed   devloped   developped   _____

Adding "ed" to Verbs *(cont.)*

Paint Can Word Sort

Think about forming the past tense to each of these words. Then write each one in its past tense form on the correct paint can.

equip	develop	prepare	slip	nod
arrive	happen	decide	rub	laugh
snap	finish	require	pass	raise

Just Add "d"

Add "ed"

Double Final Consonant Add "ed"

grinned

Adding "ed" to Verbs that End in "y"

Here are a few rules to follow when making a verb that ends in "y" past tense:

- To form the past tense, add "-ed" to a verb (action word).
- If the verb ends with a consonant followed by a "y," drop the "y" and add "-ied."
- Simply add "-ed" if the verb ends with a vowel followed by a "y."

Word	Base + Ending	In Context
tried	try + ed	I **tried** to explain what had happened.
cried	cry + ed	The baby **cried** even louder.
replied	reply + ed	The man **replied** to the letter quickly.
hurried	hurry + ed	She **hurried** toward the bus stop.
married	marry + ed	They got **married** 20 years ago.
buried	bury + ed	The pirate **buried** the chest full of gold coins.
classified	classify + ed	Check the newspaper's **classified** ads for what you want.
occupied	occupy + ed	The seat was **occupied**.
satisfied	satisfy + ed	The teacher was **satisfied** with Tonya's report.
enjoyed	enjoy + ed	The children **enjoyed** singing.
destroyed	destroy + ed	The man tore down the poster and **destroyed** it.
employed	employ + ed	She is **employed** at a fast food place.
annoyed	annoy + ed	I get **annoyed** when people play music way too loud.
sprayed	spray + ed	The girl **sprayed** the water on her brother.
obeyed	obey + ed	The boy **obeyed** his mother.

Choose the best word from the list above to complete each sentence. Write it on the line. Use each word once. Skip those you can't figure out and return to them once you've done the others.

1. He is _____ to Sue.

2. Matt's tower of bricks was _____ when Todd tripped and fell.

3. Her dog _____ her every command.

4. A car already _____ my parking spot.

5. The girl _____ to catch the school bus.

6. They _____ listening to country music.

7. Although the women _____ to fight the fire, it spread rapidly.

8. Did you see a skateboard ramp for sale in the paper's _____ ads?

9. She _____ to his question as soon as she knew the answer.

10. He _____ the cleaner on the tub.

11. The answer the witness gave hadn't _____ the judge.

12. The company _____ about 500 people.

13. I've always hoped to find _____ treasure.

14. Dad was _____ that we took so long to get ready to go.

15. The baby _____ for most of the afternoon.

Adding "ed" to Verbs that End in "y" *(cont.)*

Using a Dictionary

Write each spelling word. Look up each one in a dictionary. What are the two guide words at the top of the page? Write the guide words.

Spelling Word	Left-Side Guide Word	Right-Side Guide Word
ex. stayed	state	stead
1.		
2.		
3.		
4.		
5.		
6.		
7.		
8.		
9.		
10.		
11.		
12.		
13.		
14.		
15.		

Adding "ing" to Verbs

Here are a few rules to follow adding "ing" to a verb:
- The letters "ing" are added to a verb (action word).
- If the word ends with an "e," drop the "e" and add "ing."
- If the final letters in the word are a short vowel followed by a single consonant, double the consonant and add "ing."
- A one-syllable word ending in "ie" will change to "y" before adding the "ing."

Word	Base + Ending	In Context
burning	burn + ing	The barn was already **burning** when we got there.
breaking	break + ing	The men were **breaking** the rules.
feeling	feel + ing	I've been **feeling** ill today.
giving	give + ing	What are you **giving** him for his birthday?
exciting	excit + ing	We had an **exciting** time at the birthday party.
shining	shine + ing	Yesterday the sun was **shining**.
diving	dive + ing	A girl was **diving** into the deep water.
amazing	amaze + ing	The team did some **amazing** magic tricks for us.
admitting	admit + ing	I'm **admitting** that I did the wrong thing.
winning	win + ing	You must be on a **winning** streak.
grabbing	grab + ing	The baby started **grabbing** his sister's toys.
begging	beg + ing	My kids have been **begging** to go to an amusement park.
tying	tie + ing	The woman started **tying** a rope around her waist.
dying	die + ing	The flowers were all **dying** due to the lack of rain.
lying	lie + ing	There's no sense in **lying** about it.

Copy the spelling words in the order they appear above. Number them in order from A–Z. You may need to look as far as the third letter. Then write the words in A–Z order.

Word Number	Number	A-Z Order
1.		
2.		
3.		
4.		
5.		
6.		
7.		
8.		
9.		
10.		
11.		
12.		
13.		
14.		
15.		

Adding "ing" to Verbs *(cont.)*

Writing Questions and Answers

Write a short question using each of your spelling words. Then write an answer using the spelling word again. You will use most of the words from your question in your answer.

Question	Answer
ex. Did you go **swimming** today?	Yes, we did go **swimming** today.
1.	
2.	
3.	
4.	
5.	
6.	
7.	
8.	
9.	
10.	
11.	
12.	
13.	
14.	
15.	

Plurals

Here are a few rules about plurals:
- Plurals show more than one.
- Usually you do this by adding "s" to the end of the word.
- However, if the word ends in "s," "o," "x," "z," "ch" or "sh," you must add "es."

Word	Base + Ending	In Context
friends	friend + s	He has six **friends** in that class.
answers	answer + s	She knew all the **answers** to the test questions.
sentences	sentence + s	The teacher said to write at least six **sentences**.
weddings	wedding + s	I have three **weddings** to attend this month.
minutes	minute + s	After about ten **minutes**, the taxi arrived.
buses	bus + es	Four **buses** passed me before one stopped.
glasses	glass + es	I filled three **glasses** with milk.
addresses	address + es	The book contains people's names and **addresses**.
potatoes	potato + es	Mom bought a five-pound sack of **potatoes**.
mosquitoes	mosquito + es	We had to come inside because **mosquitoes** were biting us.
boxes	box + es	The **boxes** spilled out from beneath the Christmas tree.
branches	branch + es	The tree's **branches** broke under the weight of the ice.
sandwiches	sandwich + es	Please fix us some peanut butter **sandwiches**.
dishes	dish + es	I'll put these **dishes** on the table.
bushes	bush + es	Let's plant some **bushes** in that corner of the yard.

Write each spelling word on the correct line in column two. Then, in column three, show which letters need to be added to make the word plural and why.

Singular	Plural	Reason Plural Appears this Way
ex. table	tables	add "s" to show more than one
ex. tomato	tomatoes	add "es" to words ending with "o"
1. bush		
2. friend		
3. potato		
4. dish		
5. minute		
6. sentence		
7. sandwich		
8. address		
9. mosquito		
10. branch		
11. wedding		
12. box		
13. answer		
14. bus		
15. glass		

Plurals (cont.)

Crossword Puzzle

Choose the spelling word that would best complete each clue.

Across

2. Their _____ were held on the same day.
6. I can only wait for about six more _____ ; then I've got to leave.
7. One of his favorite things to eat is mashed _____ and gravy.
8. Our class planted some _____ along the sidewalk.
10. Due to the icy conditions, all of the school _____ were late that morning.
13. Please write the _____ on these envelopes.
14. They're having several different kinds of _____ at their family picnic.

Down

1. I know you have lots of questions, but I don't have any _____ .
3. Writing spelling words in _____ is a good way to practice.
4. The _____ fell off the table and shattered.
5. The town sprays this area to cut down on the number of _____ .
8. When the mail carrier tripped, she dropped the _____ she'd been carrying.
9. How many _____ do you plan on inviting to your birthday party?
11. She trimmed the tree's lower _____ .
12. Please wash and dry this stack of dirty _____ .

Plurals when Nouns End in "y"

Here are a few rules about plurals:
- Plurals show more than one.
- If the word ends in a vowel and a "y," just add "s."
- If the word ends in a consonant and a "y," drop the "y" and add "ies."

Word	Base + Ending	In Context
holidays	holiday + s	Where are you spending the **holidays**?
highways	highway + s	The snow plows always clean major **highways** first.
displays	display + s	The store's window **displays** were very colorful.
birthdays	birthday + s	Both girls have **birthdays** during the month of February.
donkeys	donkey + s	Three **donkeys** lived in the tiny shed.
surveys	survey + s	All of the television stations sent **surveys** to their viewers.
cowboys	cowboy + s	In the movie two **cowboys** fell off their horses.
guys	guy + s	Where are you **guys** going?
colonies	colony + es	The American **colonies** demanded freedom from Britain.
butterflies	butterfly + es	Monarch **butterflies** are yellow and black.
mysteries	mystery + es	Some **mysteries** may never be solved.
activities	activity + es	We had many **activities** for the children to do at the party.
berries	berry + es	Many vitamins are found in **berries**.
factories	factory + es	The fire damaged two **factories**.
stories	story + es	I always enjoy hearing your **stories**.

Write each spelling word in one of the columns. A few examples have been given.

Plurals ending with "s"	Purals ending with "ies"
keys	pennies

Plurals when Nouns End in "y" *(cont.)*

Word Scramble

Unscramble the words below to form spelling words from this lesson. Put the letters on the lines below to find the answer to the riddle.

Example: bnsnuie   b   u   n   n   i   e   s
               1

1. veyssur
2. iesstor
3. daysihol
4. tivactiesi
5. usgy
6. wayshigh
7. riesber
8. boyscwo
9. faciestor
10. thbirydas
11. terfliesbut
12. laysdisp
13. kyesdon
14. iestermys
15. niescool

Riddle: Why did the golfer wear two pairs of pants?

___ ___   ___ ___ ___ ___   ___ ___ ___   ___ ___ ___ ___
8   23   11   13   14   10   7   4   16   21   5   15   3

___   ___ ___ ___ ___ ___   ___ ___   ___ ___ ___
19   9   22   17   2   18   20   12   1   6

Unusual Plurals

Here are a few rules about plurals:
- Plurals show more than one.
- Some words that end in "f" or "fe" change the "f" to a "v" and add "es" to form the plural.

Word	More than One	In Context
life	lives	People say that cats have nine **lives**, but it's not true.
wife	wives	Their **wives** met at the dinner party last month.
shelf	shelves	I need a set of **shelves** to hold all of these books.
wolf	wolves	The **wolves** howled.
loaf	loaves	He ordered two **loaves** of bread from the bakery.
leaf	leaves	After all of the **leaves** fell, we raked them.
thief	thieves	Several **thieves** carried out the crime.

Here is another rule about plurals:
- Some words do not add "s" or "es" in order to form the plural.

Word	More than One	In Context
foot	feet	I've stood in the snow for so long that my **feet** are cold.
mouse	mice	We have a pair of pet **mice**.
goose	geese	The **geese** made loud honking sounds.
crisis	crises	There have already been two **crises** today!
moose	moose	The five **moose** moved closer to the road.
person	people	Six **people** were trapped inside the building.
deer	deer	The hunters brought home three **deer**.
sheep	sheep	Four **sheep** got through the hole in the fence.

Is the **boldfaced** word spelled wrong? If it is not correct, write it correctly in the middle column. If it is right, circle **OK**.

1. Are your **feet** sore?		OK
2. The four **thiefs** went to jail.		OK
3. Please put your packages on the **shelves**.		OK
4. Six **moose** grazed in a marsh.		OK
5. The bakery made 65 **loafs** of bread each day.		OK
6. Only nine **people** showed up.		OK
7. I had a problem with **mice** in my basement.		OK
8. She especially liked plants with red **leafs**.		OK
9. The rancher owned 300 **sheep**.		OK
10. How many **crisis** have you had to handle today?		OK
11. We saw at least five **deers** in the field.		OK
12. The three **wolves** were part of a larger pack.		OK
13. Six Canadian **gooses** lived in the pond.		OK
14. The two men's **wives** were best friends.		OK
15. Three **lifes** were lost because of the storm.		OK

Unusual Plurals *(cont.)*

Draw It

Fill in the chart below with words and pictures.

Word for One	Draw One	Word for Two	Draw Two
ex. calf		calves	
1. goose			
2. sheep			
3. thief			
4. mouse			
5. loaf			
6. foot			
7. deer			
8. wife			
9. moose			
10. shelf			
11. person			
12. leaf			
13. wolf			

14. Write the two spelling words not mentioned in the chart:

_____ and _____

Silent Letters: "mb" & "stle"

In the spelling pattern "mb," the "b" is silent.

In the spelling pattern "stle," the "t" is silent, making "stle" sound like "sull."

Word	In Context
climbed	The girl **climbed** through the window.
thumb	He hit his **thumb** with the hammer.
lamb	That **lamb** is only four days old.
combing	She spends a lot of time **combing** her hair.
plumber	The **plumber** found a toy clogging the sink drain.
bombs	Some countries use **bombs** during a war.
castle	She drew what she thought Cinderella's **castle** looked like.
trestle	The train **trestle** shook each time a train went over it.
wrestler	My brother is a **wrestler**, and he has a match today.
bristles	Both hedgehogs and porcupines are covered with **bristles**.
thistle	The mule enjoyed eating the **thistle**.
whistle	Do you know how to **whistle**?
jostle	I'm sorry! I didn't mean to **jostle** you and make you drop your bag!
hustle	You'll need to **hustle** if you intend to catch that flight.
rustle	I could hear the wind **rustle** the trees' leaves.

Copy the spelling words in the order they appear above. Circle the silent letter. Write the words again with the silent letter in a different color.

Circle the Silent Letter	Silent Letter in Different Color
1.	
2.	
3.	
4.	
5.	
6.	
7.	
8.	
9.	
10.	
11.	
12.	
13.	
14.	
15.	

Silent Letters: "mb" & "stle" (cont.)

Word Wheels

Write the spelling words on the spokes of the appropriate wheel.

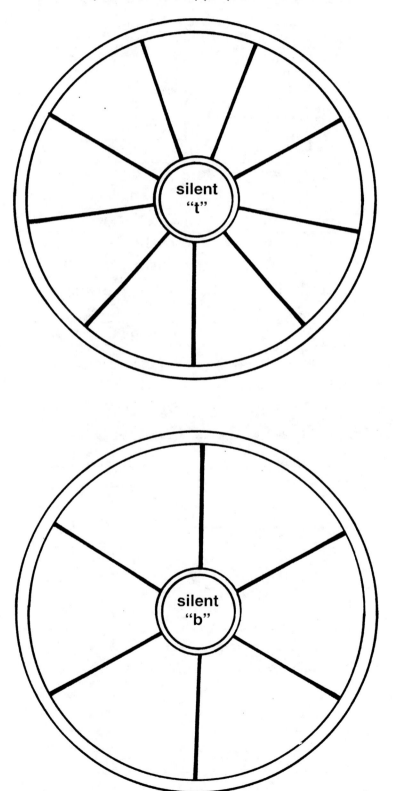

Silent Letters Spelling Pattern: "tch"

In the spelling pattern "tch," the "t" is always silent:

Word	In Context
catch	My dog got loose, and I'm trying to **catch** him.
match	Use that **match** to light the candle.
watch	Do you know where I left my **watch**?
patch	Can you please put a **patch** over this rip?
scratch	A cat may **scratch** your couch and chairs.
hatchet	The man used the **hatchet** to chop up more wood.
sketch	Here's a **sketch** of the dress I'd like you to make for me.
stretch	Will the cloth **stretch** enough to fit?
itch	The girl said that the rash made her **itch**.
witch	The **witch** had on a black cape.
switch	The light **switch** is over on that wall.
stitch	My sewing machine can do a zigzag **stitch**.
pitcher	He filled the **pitcher** with fruit punch.
kitchen	We have no dining room, so we eat in our **kitchen**.
crutches	You can get around using these **crutches**.

Copy the spelling words in the order they appear above. Then, if you can add "ed" to make a *real* word, write it in the second column. If you can add "s" or "es" to make a *real* word, write it in the third.

Spelling Word	Does adding an "ed" to the end make a *real* word?	Does adding an "s" or "es" to the end make a *real* word?
ex. latch	latched	latches
1.		
2.		
3.		
4.		
5.		
6.		
7.		
8.		
9.		
10.		
11.		
12.		
13.		
14.		
15.		

Silent Letters Spelling Pattern: "tch" *(cont.)*

Word Detective

Write the spelling word that fits the clue given. Each word is used once.

Clue	What am I?
1. I am a drawing you made.	sketch
2. I appear on your skin when a cat claws you.	
3. I turn lights on and off.	
4. I hold milk or juice.	
5. I show you the time.	
6. I help a person with a broken ankle walk.	
7. I cover up a hole in the knee of your jeans.	
8. You may do this when you first wake up.	
9. I hold fabric together.	
10. I can start a fire.	
11. You feel this after a mosquito bites you.	
12. I'm the place where people make dinner.	
13. I am a game you play with a ball.	
14. I fly on a broom and stir a cauldron.	
15. I can chop down a tree.	

Spelling Pattern: "eig"

The spelling pattern "eig" says long /a/, as in the word "say."

Word	In Context
eight	My brother is **eight** years old.
eighth	His **eighth** birthday was last week.
freight	The **freight** train moved slowly.
weigh	How much do you **weigh**?
weight	He lost a lot of **weight** last year.
overweight	That person looks **overweight**.
paperweight	You can hold papers down with a **paperweight**.
neighbors	Our next-door **neighbors** are very nice people.
neighborhood	In the summer all the kids in the **neighborhood** play.
beige	She wore a pair of **beige** pants.
sleigh	We went for a horse-drawn **sleigh** ride.

In some cases, the letters "ei" alone say long /a/.

Word	Context
their	I think **their** daughter has brown hair.
veil	The bride wore a white **veil**.
veins	We have hundreds of **veins** in our bodies.
reindeer	Santa's **reindeer** pull his sleigh.

Choose the best word from the list above to complete each sentence. Write it on the line.
Use each word once. Skip those you can't figure out and return to them once you've done the others.

1. I met _____ son in Germany.

2. She used to _____ a lot less than she does now.

3. My next-door _____ are moving to another town.

4. A big, old-fashioned red _____ stood in front of the bed and breakfast inn.

5. There are _____ children in my family.

6. He needs an operation on the_____in his legs.

7. She put on a _____ sweater.

8. Your seats are in the _____ row from the stage.

9. Most _____ are found in cold parts of the world.

10. Our entire _____ held a street party last July.

11. Planes and trains carry large items as _____.

12. If you are _____, you may need to go on a diet.

13. The bride's _____ was so long that it reached to the ground.

14. When he lifted the _____, all the papers blew onto the floor.

15. Some people measure _____ in grams and kilograms.

Spelling Pattern: "eig" *(cont.)*

Word Scramble

Unscramble the words to form spelling words from this lesson. Put the letters on the lines below to find the answer to the riddle.

Example: ekac   <u>c</u>   <u>a</u>   <u>k</u>   <u>e</u>
                      1   2

1. deerrnei   ___ ___ ___ ___ ___ ___ ___ ___
       3

2. lieshg   ___ ___ ___ ___ ___
     4

3. treifhg   ___ ___ ___ ___ ___ ___
        5

4. rhite   ___ ___ ___ ___ ___
     6

5. verothgiew   ___ ___ ___ ___ ___ ___ ___ ___ ___ ___
            7

6. gthei   ___ ___ ___ ___ ___
      8

7. doohborniegh   ___ ___ ___ ___ ___ ___ ___ ___ ___ ___ ___ ___
                    9

8. sneiv   ___ ___ ___ ___ ___
        10

9. perwepaigth   ___ ___ ___ ___ ___ ___ ___ ___ ___ ___ ___
      11

10. eegib   ___ ___ ___ ___ ___
        12

11. whige   ___ ___ ___ ___ ___
   13

12. theigh   ___ ___ ___ ___ ___ ___
          14

13. eliv   ___ ___ ___ ___
     15

14. nigehsrob   ___ ___ ___ ___ ___ ___ ___ ___ ___
                 16

15. twigeh   ___ ___ ___ ___ ___ ___
       17

Riddle: What body of water is always wealthy?

<u>A</u> ___   ___ ___ ___ ___ ___.   ___ ___ ___   ___ ___ ___
1   7   17   15   5   3   8   6   4   12   9   6

___ ___ ___   ___ ___ ___ <u>k</u> ___
14   13   9   16   11   10   2   4

Spelling Pattern: "ect"

The spelling pattern "ect" appears within many words and is pronounced just as it's written.

Word	In Context
correct	Did you get the second question **correct**?
object	The lawyer stood up to **object** to the question.
director	The movie **director** changed the lighting.
reject	The workers **reject** any goods that aren't perfect.
elect	In the USA, we **elect** our leaders.
electric	I have an **electric** stove.
insects	This farm is sprayed to get rid of **insects**.
protect	Seat belts **protect** people during a car crash.
collect	She likes to **collect** baseball cards.
connect	You complete the puzzle when you **connect** all of the pieces.
project	When is our social studies **project** due?
select	What books did you **select**?
reflect	Whenever there's light, mirrors will **reflect**.
perfect	He got a **perfect** score.
respect	Always treat others with **respect**.

Is the **boldfaced** word spelled wrong? If it is not correct, write it correctly in the middle column. If it is right, circle **OK**.

1. The group's **director** had the idea.		OK
2. Do you think the students will **ellect** Tara?		OK
3. Your grades **reflect** the amount of effort you put in.		OK
4. Shots can **protect** you from certain diseases.		OK
5. I **colect** old vases.		OK
6. Never touch **electric** wires that are on the ground.		OK
7. Train cars **conect** to the engine.		OK
8. They'll probably **select** George as their leader.		OK
9. The **project** took longer than we expected.		OK
10. You need to **corect** your errors.		OK
11. Please **respect** my wishes.		OK
12. I think that she will **regect** his offer.		OK
13. Birds eat **insecks**.		OK
14. What is that odd-looking **object**?		OK
15. Your hair looks **prefect**.		OK

Spelling Pattern: "ect" *(cont.)*

Using a Dictionary

Copy the spelling words. Look up each one in a dictionary. What are the two guide words at the top of the page? Write the guide words.

Spelling Word	Left-Side Guide Word	Right-Side Guide Word
ex. inspect	insert	instead
1.		
2.		
3.		
4.		
5.		
6.		
7.		
8.		
9.		
10.		
11.		
12.		
13.		
14.		
15.		

Words Ending in "dle"& "ple"

At the end of a word a consonant followed by "le" rhymes with "skull." This means that "dle" sounds like "dull" and "ple" sounds like "pull."

Word	In Context
middle	A table stood in the **middle** of the room.
handle	She put her hand on the door's **handle**.
needle	Thread the **needle** with black thread.
candle	He lit the yellow **candles**.
bundle	The old lady carried a large **bundle** of clothing.
saddle	Her horse doesn't like that **saddle**.
sample	Would you like a **sample** of cheesecake?
example	Can you give me an **example**?
purple	They chose a **purple** rug.
simple	Changing a light bulb is **simple**.
dimple	He had a **dimple** in his chin.
multiple	I need **multiple** copies of this bulletin.
apple	Would you like to eat this **apple**?
couple	The **couple** set a wedding date.
maple	In the fall **maple** trees drop their leaves.

Copy the spelling words in the order they appear above. Number them in order from A–Z. Write the words in A–Z order.

Word Number	Number	A-Z Order
1.		
2.		
3.		
4.		
5.		
6.		
7.		
8.		
9.		
10.		
11.		
12.		
13.		
14.		
15.		

Words Ending in "dle" & "ple" (cont.)

Word Scale

Count the number of spelling words that end with "-dle." Count the number of spelling words that end in "-ple." Which group has more? Fill in the balance, grouping the words by their ending. **Be sure to put the group with the most words on the heavier side.**

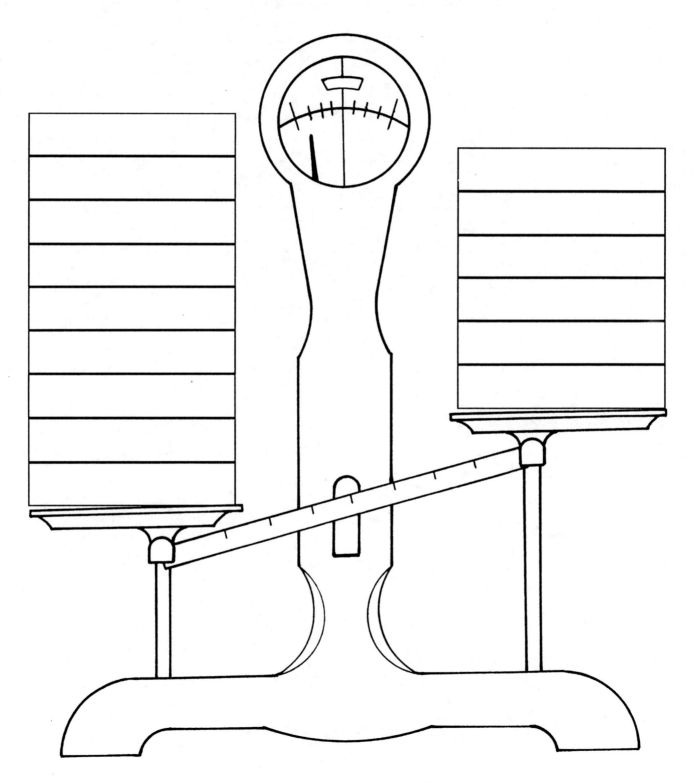

Words Ending in "tle" & "cle"

At the end of a word a consonant followed by "le" rhymes with "skull." This means that "tle" sounds like "tull," and "cle" sounds like "cull."

Word	In Context
uncle	My **uncle** is 36 years old.
article	Did you see the **article** about the new movie?
particle	A **particle** is a tiny piece, like a grain of sand.
cycle	The water **cycle** describes how water moves through the Earth's system.
bicycle	He got a new **bicycle** for a birthday gift.
icicle	The **icicle** broke off and fell from the roof.
little	The **little** girl started to cry.
cattle	The cowboys rounded up the **cattle**.
settlers	During the 1800s many **settlers** started farms in the Midwest.
bottle	The glass **bottle** broke when it fell on the floor.
battle	The **battle** raged on all day and night.
title	What's the **title** of your favorite fairy tale?
turtle	The **turtle** ducked its head under the water.
shuttle	A **shuttle** moved people between the parking area and the festival.
rattlesnake	The **rattlesnake** was coiled and ready to strike.

Circle the word that's spelled correctly. Copy it on the line.

1. uncal   uncle   unkle   _____

2. bicycle   bicicle   bycicle   _____

3. partical   pratical   particle   _____

4. tertle   turtle   turtel   _____

5. battle   battel   batle   _____

6. litle   littel   little   _____

7. settlers   setlers   seddlers   _____

8. rattlsnake   rattlesnake   ratlesnake   _____

9. icycle   icycel   icicle   _____

10. cycle   cicyle   ciycle   _____

11. artical   article   articel   _____

12. title   titel   tittle   _____

13. botle   bottel   bottle   _____

14. shuttle   shuttel   shutle   _____

15. catle   cattle   cattel   _____

Words Ending in "tle" & "cle" *(cont.)*

Crossword Puzzle

Choose the spelling word that would best complete each clue.

Across

3. My father's brother is my _____ .
4. The baby dropped its _____ and started to cry.
5. Last winter, the dripping water formed a large _____ .
7. I was afraid of the _____ lying on a rock in the sun.
10. You must clean it until every _____ of dust is gone.
12. She plans to _____ her latest book *Journey Out of Darkness*.
14. Seasons change each year in a specific _____ .
15. The clown gave the balloon to the _____ child.

Down

1. The man put together the _____ and put it under the Christmas tree.
2. The space _____ took astronauts to fix the satellite.
6. Have you read that news _____ about electric cars?
8. The white _____ and the Native Americans sometimes had fights.
9. The first real _____ of the Revolutionary War occurred at Lexington.
11. The rancher branded all of the _____ with a capital V.
13. Kaylee's pet _____ hides in its shell most of the time.

More "le" Word Endings

At the end of a word a consonant followed by "le" rhymes with "skull." This means that "gle" sounds like "gull," "fle" sounds like "full," "kle" sounds like "kull," and "zle" sounds like "zull."

Word	In Context
angle	A picture on the wall hung at a crazy **angle**.
single	He fired a **single** shot.
triangle	A **triangle** has three sides.
jungle	It was hot and humid in the **jungle**.
rectangle	A **rectangle** has four sides.
eagle	The **eagle** swooped down to catch its prey.
rifle	The sound of the **rifle** made the horse gallop across the field.
shuffle	Please **shuffle** the cards before dealing them.
sniffle	I didn't have a tissue, so I had to **sniffle**.
waffle	He ate a large **waffle** topped with apples for breakfast.
chuckle	They heard the child **chuckle**.
ankle	He hurt his **ankle** in the crash.
sprinkle	We used the hose to **sprinkle** water on the garden.
puzzle	Can you help me finish this **puzzle**?
sizzle	The bacon began to **sizzle** in the frying pan.

Copy the spelling words in the order they appear above. If it's a noun (person, place, or thing), write its plural form. If it's a verb (action word), add an "s." Then write a short sentence using the spelling word's new form.

Word	Add "s"	Sentence Using New Form
ex. baffle	baffles	This mystery baffles me.
1.		
2.		
3.		
4.		
5.		
6.		
7.		
8.		
9.		
10.		
11.		
12.		
13.		
14.		
15.		

More "le" Word Endings *(cont.)*

Pairs of Boots

Add **"fle,"** **"gle,"** **"kle,"** or **"zle"** to each boot to form a word. Then write the spelling word formed by the pair.

1.
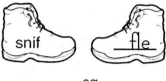 

_____ sniffle _____

2.

_____

3.

_____

4.
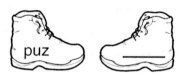

_____

5.

_____

6.

_____

7.
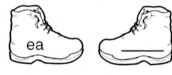

_____

8.

_____

9.

_____

10.
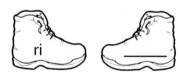

_____

11.

_____

12.

_____

13.

_____

14.

_____

15.
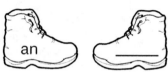

_____

Word Ending: "al"

The word ending "al" says "ull," the same sound as in "skull."

Word	In Context
animal	An **animal** was caught in the trap.
several	The cut was **several** inches long.
metal	Recycle your **metal** cans.
natural	The Grand Canyon is a place with a lot of **natural** beauty.
capital	The **capital** of the U.S.A. is Washington, D.C.
total	The **total** cost is $168.
original	Is this the **original** box that the toy came in?
signal	Turn left at the next **signal** light.
central	That store is in the **central** part of the mall.
local	You won't have to pay if it's a **local** call.
federal	It is a **federal** law.
normal	The **normal** temperature for this time of year is much warmer.
practical	It's not **practical** to drive so far in one day.
hospital	The woman hurried to the **hospital**.
musical	Have you ever played **musical** chairs?

Copy the spelling words in the order they appear above. Number them in order from A–Z. Write the words in A–Z order.

Word Number	Number	A-Z Order
1.		
2.		
3.		
4.		
5.		
6.		
7.		
8.		
9.		
10.		
11.		
12.		
13.		
14.		
15.		

Word Ending: "al" (cont.)

Word Chain

Write each spelling word inside a link of this chain.

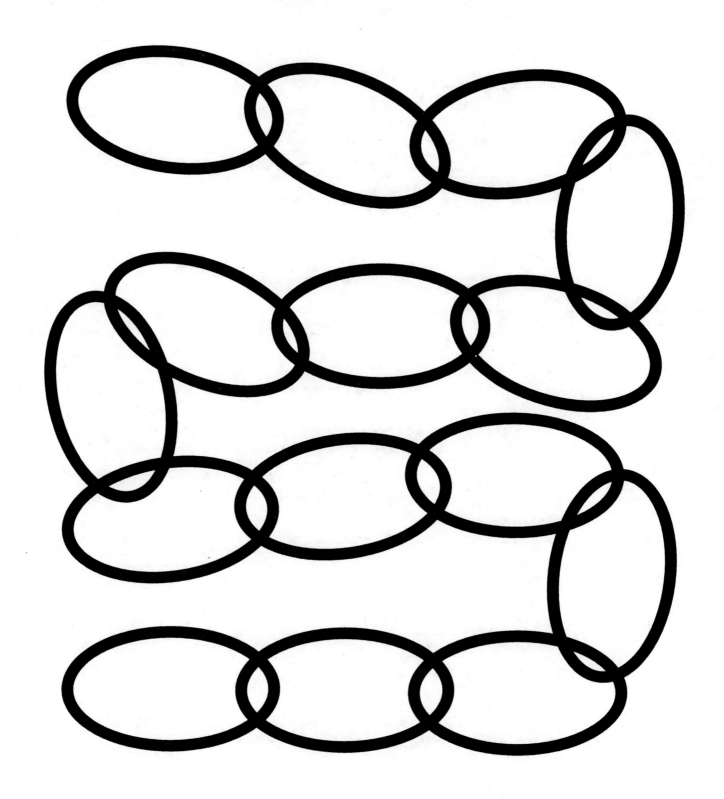

Word Ending: "dge"

The letters "dge" often come at the end of a word and do not make the sound of any of the letters. Instead "dge" says the "j" sound:

Word	The In Context
badge	The police officer showed her **badge** to the man.
gadget	My mom invents a new **gadget** almost every week.
edge	The pencil fell over the table's **edge**.
ledge	The child was too close to the **ledge**.
pledge	We signed a **pledge** to never take drugs.
wedge	The glass of ice water had a lime **wedge** at the top.
ridge	The installers had to come back to fix the **ridge** in the carpeting.
bridge	There's only one **bridge** across the river.
lodge	Although it was almost hidden by the trees, I found the old stone **lodge**.
fudge	My grandmother makes the world's best **fudge**.
grudge	It's not wise to hold a **grudge** against another person.
budget	If you **budget** well, you will have some money to save and some to spend.
smudge	Please wipe that **smudge** off the window
judge	The woman was voted the new family court **judge**.
nudged	I **nudged** my brother with my elbow.

Copy the spelling words in the first column in the order they appear above. Circle the word part "dge." Then write the words again with the "dge" word part in a different color.

Circle the Word Part	Word Part in Different Color
1.	
2.	
3.	
4.	
5.	
6.	
7.	
8.	
9.	
10.	
11.	
12.	
13.	
14.	
15.	

Word Ending: "dge" *(cont.)*

Finding Synonyms

Look up each spelling word in a dictionary or a thesaurus (if available). Find its synonym (word that means almost the same thing). Then write each spelling word on the line next to its synonym(s). A few show several synonyms to help you choose the best word.

Synonym(s)	Spelling Word
1. amount of money you can spend	
2. crest of the mountain	
3. shelf	
4. crossing	
5. candy	
6. rim	
7. tool	
8. cabin	
9. smear	
10. identification	
11. elbowed	
12. oath	
13. spite; envy	
14. piece; often triangular	
15. evaluate	

Word Ending: "ly"

The word ending "ly" says "lee." These letters are often used to change a word into an adverb. Adverbs tell how something is done: running quickly; finally finished; grasped firmly.

Word	In Context
daily	The store is open **daily** from 10 a.m. to 8 p.m.
gently	The girl **gently** laid the doll down.
usually	I **usually** get up at 7:30 a.m.
early	Today, I had to get up **early**.
finally	The movie **finally** ended at midnight.
quickly	The boy **quickly** crossed the room and opened the door.
suddenly	They **suddenly** realized that they were not alone.
probably	You **probably** left the keys at home.
exactly	There are **exactly** 23 children in Mrs. Vale's class.
rapidly	Daylight was fading **rapidly**.
firmly	She held her dog's leash **firmly**.
immediately	He called the doctor **immediately**.
frequently	We visit the city **frequently**.
lovely	She looked **lovely** in her red gown.
gradually	The wind **gradually** died down.

Circle the word that's spelled correctly. Copy it on the line.

1. finaly   finnally   finally   _____

2. exactly   exatly   exackly   _____

3. imediately   immedately   immediately   _____

4. erly   early   earlly   _____

5. gradally   gradualy   gradually   _____

6. fimly   firmly   fermly   _____

7. lovely   lovly   lovelly   _____

8. quikly   quicly   quickly   _____

9. rapidlly   rapidly   rappidly   _____

10. usually   usualy   ussually   _____

11. suddenly   sudenly   suddennly   _____

12. frequantly frequntly   frequently   _____

13. probly   probably   probaby   _____

14. dayly   dailly   daily   _____

15. gently   gentley   jently   _____

Word Ending: "ly" *(cont.)*

Finding Antonyms

Copy each spelling word. Look up each spelling word in a dictionary or a thesaurus. Decide what its antonym would be (a word with the opposite meaning). Choose the antonym(s) from the box and write them next to the correct word. Some antonyms will be used multiple times. A number indicates how many antonyms for each spelling word.

roughly	quickly	rapidly	rarely*	slowly*	nightly
unlikely	first	late	softly	ugly	gradually*
approximately					

*This antonym is used more than once.

Spelling Word	Antonym(s)
ex. happily	(1) sadly
1.	(1)
2.	(1)
3.	(1)
4.	(1)
5.	(1)
6.	(2)
7.	(2)
8.	(1)
9.	(1)
10.	(2)
11.	(1)
12.	(2)
13.	(1)
14.	(1)
15.	(2)

Find the spelling words that share antonyms. These spelling words are synonyms. This means that they have similar meanings and are sometimes used in place of each other; for example: happily and joyfully. For each set of synonyms, the first letters of the words have been provided. List the four synonym pairs:

16. u_____ and f_____

17. s_____ and i_____

18. s_____ and g_____

19. r_____ and q_____

Assessment 1

Read each sentence. Read all of the answers. Fill in the circle of the word that is spelled right and best completes the sentence.

1. We plan to get to the airport by five _____ .
   - ⓐ oclock
   - ⓑ o'clock
   - ⓒ o'clok

2. They _____ chickens on their farm.
   - ⓐ raised
   - ⓑ raisd
   - ⓒ raized

3. The tired girl _____ her eyes.
   - ⓐ rubed
   - ⓑ rubbd
   - ⓒ rubbed

4. The dog _____ its bone in the yard.
   - ⓐ buried
   - ⓑ baried
   - ⓒ buryed

5. He's been _____ by that firm for six years.
   - ⓐ impolyed
   - ⓑ employed
   - ⓒ employied

6. The movie was very _____ .
   - ⓐ excitng
   - ⓑ exciting
   - ⓒ exsiting

7. Many plants were _____ due to the early frost.
   - ⓐ dieing
   - ⓑ diying
   - ⓒ dying

8. My mom fixed us some turkey _____ .
   - ⓐ sandwichs
   - ⓑ sanwiches
   - ⓒ sandwiches

9. The company bought land on which it plans to build two _____ .
   - ⓐ factories
   - ⓑ factries
   - ⓒ factorys

10. She served mashed _____ with gravy.
    - ⓐ potatos
    - ⓑ potatoes
    - ⓒ potattoes

11. After reviewing the _____ , the company decided to bring out a new product.
    - ⓐ surveys
    - ⓑ survays
    - ⓒ survies

12. I've already had three _____ this week!
    - ⓐ crisises
    - ⓑ crisses
    - ⓒ crises

13. The police believe there were at least two _____ involved in the robbery.
    - ⓐ thiefs
    - ⓑ thieves
    - ⓒ theives

14. We had to call the _____ to unclog the drain.
    - ⓐ plummer
    - ⓑ plumer
    - ⓒ plumber

15. The train blew its _____ .
    - ⓐ whisle
    - ⓑ whistle
    - ⓒ wistle

16. If you _____ , you'll make it worse.
    - ⓐ scratch
    - ⓑ scrach
    - ⓒ skratch

17. The owl perched on the _____ .
    - ⓐ ledge
    - ⓑ lege
    - ⓒ ledje

18. She was _____ in school, earning mostly A's and B's.
    - ⓐ sucessful
    - ⓑ succesful
    - ⓒ successful

19. He went over to visit his _____ .
    - ⓐ nabors
    - ⓑ neighbors
    - ⓒ neighers

20. An _____ broke free and fell to the ground.
    - ⓐ icle
    - ⓑ icicle
    - ⓒ icycle

Assessment 2

Darken the circle of the one word that is spelled correctly in each row. Read all of the choices before selecting one.

1. (a) February   (b) Febuary   (c) Febuery
2. (a) threwout   (b) thoroughout   (c) throughout
3. (a) shreed   (b) shred   (c) shread
4. (a) skeem   (b) sceam   (c) scheme
5. (a) squirm   (b) squerm   (c) skirm
6. (a) straght   (b) straight   (c) straiht
7. (a) splended   (b) splendid   (c) splindid
8. (a) pitcher   (b) picher   (c) pichur
9. (a) beije   (b) beige   (c) baige
10. (a) directer   (b) derector   (c) director
11. (a) cunnect   (b) conect   (c) connect
12. (a) multiple   (b) multipal   (c) multaple
13. (a) cuple   (b) couple   (c) coupal
14. (a) artical   (b) articul   (c) article
15. (a) chucle   (b) chuckle   (c) chukle
16. (a) gadget   (b) gajet   (c) gaget
17. (a) recangle   (b) retangle   (c) rectangle
18. (a) popular   (b) populer   (c) populur
19. (a) dolars   (b) dollars   (c) dollers
20. (a) probly   (b) probaby   (c) probably
21. (a) imediately   (b) immedately   (c) immediately
22. (a) aweful   (b) awful   (c) awefull
23. (a) practical   (b) practicle   (c) practecal
24. (a) originul   (b) originel   (c) original
25. (a) ansers   (b) answers   (c) anwsers
26. (a) screech   (b) screach   (c) skreech
27. (a) prepared   (b) prepaired   (c) prepard
28. (a) admiting   (b) admmitting   (c) admitting
29. (a) vail   (b) veil   (c) veigl
30. (a) hospital   (b) hospitle   (c) hospatle

Answer Key

page 4
1. OK
2. OK
3. o'clock
4. OK
5. OK
6. February
7. OK
8. decade
9. OK
10. September
11. century
12. OK
13. OK
14. January
15. July

page 5

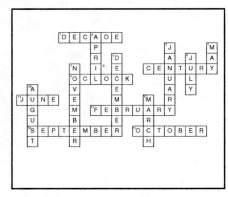

page 6
about: throughout; sprout
fed: thread, spread, shred
limp: shrimp
blink: shrink
goat: throat
loose: spruce
drain: sprain
clubs: shrubs
blew: through
spill: thrill
crawl: sprawl
peek: shriek

page 7
1. throat
2. spruce
3. sprout
4. spread
5. shrimp
6. sprain
7. thread
8. shriek
9. shred
10. thrill
11. shrubs
12. sprawl
13. through
14. shrink
15. throughout
Riddle: All the shooting stars!

page 8
1. split; slit; no
2. splash; wash; yes
3. splinter; winter; no
4. splendid; spleen; yes
5. strong; among; yes
6. string; strung; yes
7. strange; range; no
8. stream; steam; no
9. strike; bike; no
10. stress; less; no
11. stripes; strips; yes
12. street; meet; no
13. struggle; straggle; yes
14. straight; eight; no
15. strength; length; no

page 9
1. splinter
2. street
3. string
4. stress
5. straight
6. strong
7. stream
8. stripes
9. struggle
10. splash
11. splendid
12. strike
13. strength
14. split
15. strange

page 10
1. scream
2. squeal
3. screech
4. squirrel
5. scrub
6. scraps
7. squeeze
8. scheme
9. schedule
10. screen
11. squirt
12. squeak
13. scribble
14. squirm
15. scrambled

page 11
1. squeeze
2. scheme
3. squirrel
4. scribble
5. schedule
6. screech
7. squeak
8. scrub
9. squirm
10. scream
11. scraps
12. squeal
13. screen
14. scrambled
15. squirt

page 12
1. laughed
2. prepared
3. arrived
4. happened
5. required
6. raised
7. snapped
8. decided
9. nodded
10. slipped
11. finished
12. discovered
13. equipped
14. rubbed
15. developed

page 13
Words can be in any order on the cans.
"Just Add D" paint can
decided
raised
required
prepared
arrived
"Add ED" paint can
happened
laughed
developed
finished
passed
"Double Final..." paint can
snapped
nodded
slipped
rubbed
equipped

page 14
1. married
2. destroyed
3. obeyed
4. occupied
5. hurried
6. enjoyed
7. tried
8. classified
9. replied
10. sprayed
11. satisfied
12. employed
13. buried
14. annoyed
15. cried

page 15
Answers will vary based on the dictionary used.

page 16
1. burning; 5; admitting
2. breaking; 4; amazing
3. feeling; 9; begging
4. giving; 10; breaking
5. exciting; 8; burning
6. shining; 13; diving
7. diving; 6; dying
8. amazing; 2; exciting
9. admitting; 1; feeling
10. winning; 15; giving
11. grabbing; 11; grabbing
12. begging; 3; lying
13. tying; 14; shining
14. dying; 7; tying
15. lying; 12; winning

page 17
Answers will vary. It's important that the child use most of the words from the question in the response.

page 18
1. bushes; sh; es
2. friends; d; s
3. potatoes; o; es
4. dishes; sh; es
5. minutes; e; s
6. sentences; e; s
7. sandwiches; ch; es
8. addresses; s; es
9. mosquitoes; o; es
10. branches; ch; es
11. weddings; g; s
12. boxes; x; es
13. answers; r; s
14. buses; s; es
15. glasses; s; es

Answer Key (cont.)

page 19

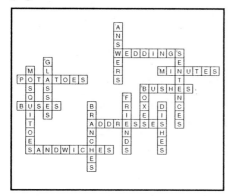

page 20

plurals ending with "s"
holidays
highways
displays
birthdays
donkeys
surveys
cowboys
guys

plurals ending with "es"
colonies
butterflies
mysteries
activities
berries
factories
stories

page 21

1. surveys
2. stories
3. holidays
4. activities
5. guys
6. highways
7. berries
8. cowboys
9. factories
10. birthdays
11. butterflies
12. displays
13. donkeys
14. mysteries
15. colonies

Riddle: In case she made a hole in one.

page 22

1. OK
2. thieves
3. OK
4. OK
5. loaves
6. OK
7. OK
8. leaves
9. OK
10. crises
11. deer
12. OK
13. geese
14. OK
15. lives

page 23

third column
1. geese
2. sheep
3. thieves
4. mice
5. loaves
6. feet
7. deer
8. wives
9. moose
10. shelves
11. people
12. leaves
13. wolves
14. crises *and* lives

page 24

1. silent letter: b
2. silent letter: b
3. silent letter: b
4. silent letter: b
5. silent letter: b
6. silent letter: b
7. silent letter: t
8. silent letter: t
9. silent letter: t
10. silent letter: t
11. silent letter: t
12. silent letter: t
13. silent letter: t
14. silent letter: t
15. silent letter: t

page 25

silent "t" wheel
castle
trestle
wrestler
bristles
thistle
whistle
jostle
hustle
rustle

silent "b" wheel
climbed
thumb
lamb
combing
plumber
bombs

page 26

1. NO; catches
2. matched; matches
3. watched; watches
4. patched; patches
5. scratched; scratches
6. NO; hatchets
7. sketched; sketches
8. stretched; stretches
9. itched; itches
10. NO; witches
11. switched; switches
12. stitched; stitches
13. NO; pitchers
14. NO; kitchens
15. NO; NO

page 27

1. sketch
2. scratch
3. switch
4. pitcher
5. watch
6. crutches
7. patch
8. stretch
9. stitch
10. match
11. itch
12. kitchen
13. catch
14. witch
15. hatchet

page 28

1. their
2. weigh
3. neighbors
4. sleigh
5. eight
6. veins
7. beige
8. eighth
9. reindeer
10. neighborhood
11. freight
12. overweight
13. veil
14. paperweight
15. weight

page 29

1. reindeer
2. sleigh
3. freight
4. their
5. overweight
6. eight
7. neighborhood
8. veins
9. paperweight
10. beige
11. weigh
12. eighth
13. veil
14. neighbors
15. weight

Riddle: A river. It's got two banks.

page 30

1. OK
2. elect
3. OK
4. OK
5. collect
6. OK
7. connect
8. OK
9. OK
10. correct
11. OK
12. reject
13. insects
14. OK
15. perfect

page 31

Answers will vary based on dictionary used.

page 32

1. middle; 9; apple
2. handle; 7; bundle
3. needle; 11; candle
4. candle; 3; couple
5. bundle; 2; dimple
6. saddle; 13; example

Answer Key *(cont.)*

7. sample; 14; handle
8. example; 6; maple
9. purple; 12; middle
10. simple; 15; multiple
11. dimple; 5; needle
12. multiple; 10; purple
13. apple; 1; saddle
14. couple; 4; sample
15. maple; 8; simple

page 33

Written on lowered side of scale:
sample
example
purple
simple
dimple
multiple
apple
couple
maple

Written on raised side of scale:
middle
handle
needle
candle
bundle
saddle

page 34

1. uncle
2. bicycle
3. particle
4. turtle
5. battle
6. little
7. settlers
8. rattlesnake
9. icicle
10. cycle
11. article
12. title
13. bottle
14. shuttle
15. cattle

page 35

page 36

Third column answers will vary. Second
column answers:

1. angles
2. singles
3. triangles
4. jungles
9. sniffles
10. waffles
11. chuckles
12. ankles

5. rectangles
6. eagles
7. rifles
8. shuffles
13. sprinkles
14. puzzles
15. sizzles

page 37

1. sniffle
2. chuckle
3. single
4. puzzle
5. angle OR ankle
6. sprinkle
7. eagle
8. waffle
9. jungle
10. rifle
11. rectangle
12. shuffle
13. ankle OR angle
14. triangle
15. sizzle

page 38

1. animal; 1; animal
2. several; 13; capital
3. metal; 7; central
4. natural; 9; federal
5. capital; 2; hospital
6. total; 15; local
7. original; 11; metal
8. signal; 14; musical
9. central; 3; natural
10. local; 6; normal
11. federal; 4; original
12. normal; 10; practical
13. practical; 12; several
14. hospital; 5; signal
15. musical; 8; total

page 40

Circled/colored part of all words is "d."

page 41

1. budget
2. ridge
3. ledge
4. bridge
5. fudge
6. edge
7. gadget
8. lodge
9. smudge
10. badge
11. nudged
12. pledge
13. grudge
14. wedge
15. judge

page 42

1. finally
2. exactly
9. rapidly
10. usually

3. immediately
4. early
5. gradually
6. firmly
7. lovely
8. quickly
11. suddenly
12. frequently
13. probably
14. daily
15. gently

page 43

in the antonym column

1. nightly
2. roughly
3. rarely
4. late
5. first
6. slowly, gradually
7. slowly, gradually
8. unlikely
9. approximately
10. slowly, gradually
11. softly
12. slowly, gradually
13. rarely
14. ugly
15. rapidly & quickly
16. usually & frequently
17. suddenly & immediately
18. rapidly & quickly
19. slowly & gradually

page 44

1. b
2. a
3. c
4. a
5. b
6. b
7. c
8. c
9. a
10. b
11. a
12. c
13. b
14. c
15. b
16. a
17. a
18. c
19. b
20. b

page 45

1. a
2. c
3. b
4. c
5. a
6. b
7. b
8. a
9. b
10. c
11. c
12. a
13. b
14. c
15. b
16. a
17. c
18. a
19. b
20. c
21. c
22. b
23. a
24. c
25. b
26. a
27. a
28. c
29. b
30. a